"LoveNotes for Lovers" can move your relationships in the direction of acceptance, understanding, fulfillment and unconditional love.

Dr. John Gray, Ph.D., Author
Men Are From Mars, Women Are From Venus &
Mars and Venus in the Bedroom

"LoveNotes for Lovers" are like the words from the songs of angels, sent from heaven to earth, enriching us with healthy messages of Love.

Dr. Larry Losoncy, Ph.D.
Marriage/Family Therapist

Also by Larry James

Books:

How to *Really* Love the One You're With
  Affirmative Guidelines for a Healthy Love Relationship

The First Book of Life$kills
  10 Ways to Maximize Your Personal and Professional
  Potential

Audio Cassette Programs:

Life$kills: The Cassette

How to *Really* Love the One You're With
  A 12-week Course in Relationship Enrichment
    Co-authored with Dr. Larry Losoncy, Ph.D.

LoveNotes for Lovers

Words That Make Music For Two Hearts Dancing!

LARRY JAMES

LoveNotes for Lovers

Words That Make Music For Two Hearts Dancing!

A Career Assurance Book ~ First Edition

Copyright © MCMXCV ~ Larry James

LoveNotes. . .™ & LoveShop™ are registered
trademarks of Larry James

This book is designed to provide accurate and authoritative
information in regard to the subject matter covered. It is sold
with the understanding that the publisher and the author are not
engaged in rendering psychological, medical, or other professional
services. If expert assistance or counseling is needed, the services
of a competent professional should be sought and is
recommended.

Printed in the United States of America
Library of Congress Catalog Card Number: 95-92143
ISBN 1-881558-03-7

Cover Design ~ Jim Weems, Ad Graphics,
Tulsa, Oklahoma ~ 800 368-6196

Distribution in the United States and Canada by
Login Publishers Consortium ~ 800 626-4330

Published by:
Career Assurance Press, P.O. Box 12695
Scottsdale, AZ 85267-2695 ~ 800 725-9223
Publisher of Books Designed to Enhance Your Personal and Business Relationships!

Contents

Dedication

A toast!

"Here's to Dr. Larry Losoncy, Ph.D., Marriage/Family Therapist, whose interest in my work has offered encouragement and
inspiration to continue my own personal inquiry into what it takes
to have a healthy love relationship with myself and others, and to
share the insights I discover. His professional critique of my
work has rendered an invaluable service to myself and those who
choose to read my books and attend our Relationship Enrichment LoveShops. He is my dear friend and colleague. I honor
his willingness to share without condition. He is loved. . . unconditionally!"

"Here's to Sandy Charveze, forever on an accelerated personal
and spiritual journey. Observing her giant step into the future
inspired meaningful conversations that have assisted me on my
own path. Her first step was taken while she was still afraid.
She has been an inspiration for many of the LoveNotes found in
this first edition. I honor her willingness to experience vulner-
ability. She is loved. . . unconditionally!"

Introduction

A satisfying love relationship is one of the most rewarding aspects of our humanity. Even love partners who view themselves as people who are in good relationships know that to choose to be in a relationship where the romance continues; where love abounds, requires constant attention to the relationship.

Love partners with open minds know that their love relationship can always be better.

From my point of view, all there is, is relationships! **LoveNotes for Lovers** is about relationships. Relationships are about how we relate; with ourselves; with our love partner (wife, husband or lover); with people; with the predicaments we find ourselves in; with our boss; with everything! How we do that, can inspire a lifetime of love with an abundance of passion and excitement or a lifetime of regret for not having lived life to its fullest in the relationships we cherish most.

Each **LoveNote** is designed to assist those who are willing to be challenged to be the best they can be for themselves and for their love partner. It will never be any easier then now, to begin to openly discuss the things we have concerns about; the things we know need to be talked about. It takes courage and the willingness to be vulnerable in your love relationship.

It has been my experience that while all of us face relationship issues, many of us resist being willing to be confronted by them. Often the thoughts presented in **LoveNotes** are overlooked and conversations about them avoided because of our preconceived notions about their importance, relevance or because of our own inability to be willing to be confronted by a relationship topic that might require us to do something different or give up being right. Can you imagine the amount of energy we expend by withholding what we are afraid to talk about? "Pass the courage, please!"

It is also my experience that we all wrestle with the same relationship issues in different ways, at different times and at different levels. This is confirmed over and over again by the participants in my Relationship Enrichment LoveShops. Each LoveShop is a place where people who are committed to having excellence in their relationships can freely and openly discuss the various pieces of the relationship puzzle in an environment of unconditional love. It is often in our most vulnerable moments that insight shares its helpful secrets.

Being willing to self-inquire when specific issues surface and to communicate our concerns about them in a loving way are prerequisites to having a great relationship with the one we love. It takes healthy attitudes to make love relationships work.

LoveNotes for Lovers was written with the hope that each **LoveNote** will inspire meaningful - though often difficult to have - conversations that will empower you to stay committed to always paying attention to your relationship; with yourself *and* with your love partner.

It is hoped that **LoveNotes** will spark desire and ignite passion; that they will inspire you to a deeper level of satisfaction while experiencing yourself and your love partner becoming more intimate in your shared experience of unconditional love.

It is my prayer that **LoveNotes for Lovers** will assist you in your own personal and spiritual journey toward healthy love relationships and in becoming a specialist in matters of the Heart.

Celebrate Love!

Larry James
Scottsdale, Arizona

LoveNotes
for
Lovers

Words That Make Music For
Two Hearts Dancing!

LARRY JAMES

LoveNote... It's the heart afraid of breaking that
never learns to dance.

From the song, "The Rose."

LoveNote. . . Words of love make the music of the heart. They resonate love and cause my heart to dance. "My heart is dancing! Come and teach it how to sing! The song of love is all there is to sing!"

LoveNote. . . One of the secrets to a healthy love relationship is to never take more than you give.

LoveNote. . . We use reasons to explain away why we don't want to do something different; reasons why we don't want to change. If we know that doing something different might help the situation, not doing something different is called "stupid." The best reason why has never solved the problem. Often reasons why are understandable, however what is not understandable is why we feel the need to have our lives dominated by reasons why we didn't do something different instead of results. When we make the decision to go for results in our love relationships. . . that's the real moment we make a decision to grow and prosper.

LoveNote... *For Singles Only* ~ If a healthy love re-lationship seems to always escape you, change your strategy. Instead of looking for love, spend more of your time breaking through the barrier you have built around your heart that keeps love from find-ing you. This barrier represents the things you are doing that may need to be examined before the voice of your heart can speak the words necessary to bring the barrier down. The only way out of this dilemma is through the barrier. No one can do this for you. Manage your thinking to look at it as a bridge you must cross, not a cross you must bear.

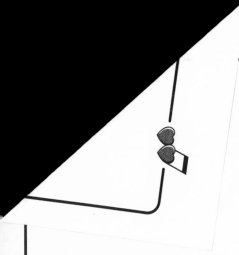

LoveNote. . . Whenever you become angry you are given the choice to challenge the anger or to surrender to it. Anger loses its power and you are empowered each time you challenge it. You have the power to transform the energy of anger to a constructive experience of release; a letting go of an emotion that can stifle your potential for personal and spiritual growth.

LoveNote. . . *Affirmation* ~ I listen when my lover shares, without making judgments. My heart is always open to hear what my love partner has to say.

LoveNote. . . We are strongest when we are letting go of what doesn't work. When we open our mind to behave in a different way, we create the freedom to love. To open our hearts to love is perhaps the greatest gift we can give to ourselves.

LoveNote... Love and verbal or physical abuse are incompatible. Someone who says they love you and continues to abuse you only thinks they need you. The truth is they will squeeze the life out of the relationship. The outcome is predictable. The person who intimidates with threats in one breath and attempts to persuade with promises of undying love the next is emotionally and mentally unstable. The sick have forgotten how to be well. Courage is called for. Refuse to become a part of the illness. Recognize its red flags. Distance yourself from such a person and seek help for yourself.

LoveNote. . . Remember to flirt with your lover, the way you did when you first met. Toss out those subtle little signals that tell your lover you are still interested; signals that show you remember the real magic that lit the fire in the beginning.

LoveNote. . . When you feel a disagreement coming on, think twice or more, before you speak what you feel to your love partner. Angry words, once spoken, reverberate like bells in a cathedral steeple. Remember, you can't un-ring a bell.

LoveNote... *For Singles Only* ~ Some of our most clear thinking about relationships can be when we are not in a relationship. Our mind is often sharper when informed by our own feelings. We are more humble and acutely more in touch with the hurts of the past. We are far more open to new ideas.

LoveNote... Never argue with your love partner's feelings. That is one argument you will always lose. Only seek to understand for what reason he or she feels that way. Learn to appreciate and respect your lover's different point of view. When it comes to feelings, no one is wrong.

RedHot LoveNote. . . When you first met your lover, the hormones were dancing! There was a fire below. Then. . . what happened? Over time, they say, the romance disappears. It doesn't have to be that way. It takes work; an awareness that to have the romance continue, you both must have an intention for it to be that way and do whatever it takes for romance to continue to be present. Being attentive to your lover's needs is a more mature level of love. It's not as if the hormones are no longer dancing. . . they are now dancing to the same music!

LoveNote. . . Only one response to conflict opens the door to intimacy; an intent to learn from the experience.

LoveNote. . . *For Women Only* ~ Be patient with your love partner when it comes to listening. Help him learn to listen by saying things worth listening to. In time he will learn how to share how he feels, openly and in a way that allows him to be vulnerable without fear. When this happens, initiate conversation that shows your appreciation of his new way of being. Patience and understanding are necessary.

LoveNote. . . You need others and you depend on yourself. Needing others is not a mistake. Giving up your responsibility for satisfying your needs is a mistake. Your need to stand alone must be tempered by your need to stand together

LoveNote. . . Always do your best to avoid, at all costs, the necessity of experiencing the negative results of anger. The healthy release of anger must be presented in a way that empowers the relationship; anger expressed without blame, without pointing fingers. To avoid unnecessary pain, it is important to learn that anger must be expressed with an attitude of acknowledgment; acknowledgment for the responsibility you have for your equal share of the upset.

RedHot LoveNote. . . Great sex is an active ingredient in a love relationship. Sex is fun and pleasure is good for you. Making love is surrendering to a higher form of energy than any one love partner can experience alone. Making love is two love partners experiencing their oneness with each other.

LoveNote. . . *For Men Only* ~ You must learn to understand the heart of a woman. When she is hurting she may say she wants you to go away. Go to her. Hold her. She doesn't need you to fix her hurt. . . only listen. Listen with understanding. . . only listen.

LoveNote. . . You can gain much insight into the power of your attitudes in the stillness of looking inward. A quiet and peaceful mind takes form as a quiet and peaceful body. Your subconscious mind believes every word you say. Your words and thoughts govern how your world and your relationship will be. Believe this and know that when problems surface; the first step is to look within. Take care to accept your share of the responsibility for the problem, then get busy doing what you can to work on the solution. Those who cannot imagine this to be true, spend most of their time and energy making sure everyone knows the problem is someone else's fault.

LoveNote... *For Singles Only* ~ You must learn to be alone and happy before you can be together with someone else and be happy. Your happiness only and always depends upon how you feel when you are alone, never how you think you will feel when you are with someone else. Healthy love relationships require that you be strong enough to resist rushing to your next relationship before all the hurts of the past are healed. Healing takes time. Doing healing alone or with the assistance of a skilled professional, will always get you where you want to go much quicker. Be alone in the short term for the extraordinary long term benefits. Learn what it takes to be in a healthy relationship with yourself. When you get comfortable with being alone; when the feeling that you must be in a relationship to feel complete disappears, most likely you will be ready for another relationship. The path to a healthy love relationship becomes more clear when you put your own well being ahead of having to be in a relationship to feel good about yourself.

LoveNote. . . If you want a healthy love relationship with committed love, without limitations, expectations, restrictions or conditions, learning to trust one another is the first step. With trust, unconditional love is possible. With unconditional love, anything is possible. God is love. With God, *nothing is impossible!*

LoveNote. . . Self-disclosure demands some risk of getting hurt. Your demonstration of courage, that is. . . revealing your true self to your love partner, in an atmosphere of unconditional love and acceptance, can open up new conversations that will support further disclosure in the most sensitive areas of your relationship, perhaps in the areas that count the most.

LoveNote. . . Maturity is the ability to harness your abilities and your energies and to do more than is expected in your relationships. The mature person refuses to settle for mediocrity. They would rather aim high and miss the mark than aim low and hit it.

LoveNote. . . You never have time to do the things you do not want to do. Remember that the next time you get bogged down in unnecessary activities that keep you from doing what you know must be done to enrich your relationship with your love partner. You always have time to do the things you want to do. Always. You always have choice. Think about it!

RedHot LoveNote. . . The spiritual connection you make with your lover when you are making love is an expression of your own spirituality. It often strengthens your commitment to be together; to really *be* together, a sacred bond. Making love with a deep commitment to one another reflects each lover's spiritual consciousness. It contributes to your spiritual survival and enhancement, as well as your physical needs. It is a promise of growth.

LoveNote. . . *For Men Only* ~ Women have a desire to be cherished and supported. It is a wise man who acknowledges this need by always doing his best to offer his support in a nurturing way. Expressing empathy, trust, acceptance, compassion and understanding all contribute to her feeling of being supported.

LoveNote. . . It is only and always fear talking when we hear a voice telling us not to get our hopes up because we will only be disappointed. Relationships can drown in negative emotions. Feelings of fear are created in our own mind. The moment fear appears; we give up our power. Feeling fearful is only an expression of a lack of love working in our relationship. Fear only surfaces when we call it up by temporarily letting go of love.

LoveNote. . . Imagine a relationship that is unimaginable; one that is so incredible that it ignites infinite possibilities. To do so is to reinvent your relationship moment by moment. The more you mentally experience the excitement of the adventure of being related, the more you will relate in committed ways that enrich and empower each other. The power of a committed relationship transforms it from one of mediocrity and complacency to one that can translate your individual intentions into the reality of a unique and truly awesome experience together.

LoveNote... The joyful expression of love produces an extraordinary freedom to create a nurturing relationship that supports individual accountability, well being, self-expression and fulfillment. *Such an exciting relationship is only possible when integrity is the foundation of the relationship.* A life together, full of passion and all the elements that encourage the full expression of unconditional love is worthy of pursuit.

LoveNote. . . Random acts of thoughtfulness keep the graceful flame of love burning. They often dazzle our lover with their brilliance. They inspire a compassionate, warm, wonderful, and loving way of being together. Our capacity to love in this way ultimately defines who we are.

LoveNote. . . There is no future in the past. Being stuck in the past serves no worthy purpose. It takes much energy to remain confused. Live in the moment. *Be* in the present. Give your all to the relationship every moment you are in it. When you give your energy to being concerned about whether your relationship will last, you are demonstrating a concern that comes from your past. This renders you unable to focus the energy you need to have your love relationship work right now. It is not possible to move forward when you are always looking backward.

LoveNote... True acceptance of your own and each other's individuality and separateness is the only foundation upon which a mature, healthy relationship can be based and from which unconditional love can grow.

LoveNote. . . Rarely is there a time when it is appropriate to withhold relevant communication in a love relationship. Communication is too important to take casually. Say what you mean. Say what you feel in a loving way and say it nevertheless. When you say what you know needs to be said, you will never have to worry about saying the wrong thing.

LoveNote... Letting go of behavioral patterns that no longer serve us often feels as though we are risking our safety and comfort. Calculated risks taken for the benefit of our own well being are worth taking. This form of movement is safer than standing still. Those who remain stationary become an easy target for misery of their own creation. The energy we expend by holding on often leaves us drained and with a feeling of hopelessness. It takes no strength to let go; only courage. Courage is a by-product of a positive self-image.

LoveNote. . . To live peacefully together in a responsible way, we must learn to understand that we are only responsible for our own individual thoughts, ideas, attitudes, decisions and actions and never for those of our love partner. To neglect our own responsibilities in the relationship in favor of our love partner's responsibility is codependency.

LoveNote... Being angry is not living in the present. Anger only represents something from our past; something that already happened. The wise thing to do is to be present to our anger; acknowledge it. Don't wallow in it. Create a new intention; to move through it. We must never allow anger to use us. Allowing anger to use us, robs us of the power we need to move forward. Instead, we must use its mighty energy to move us to the other side. There we will find only love.

LoveNote. . . *Affirmation* ~ My forever lover is also my best friend.

LoveNote. . . It is okay to say, "No." It is not okay to say, "Yes," when your heart tells you to say otherwise. It is not possible to fulfill every request made of you. Compulsively saying yes is potentially self-destructive; it is behavior that signals co-dependency. To let go of feeling guilty when you say, "No," is a new way of being that takes practice. Say 'no' to meeting the demands and needs of everyone except yourself. Stand up for you. Cease being a conspirator in your own abuse. Your relationship with someone else does not depend upon giving up yourself. You give *of* yourself to the other. You never give up yourself *to* the other. Healthy, mature love does not make us less than we are individually.

RedHot LoveNote. . . Touching enlivens our lives. It nurtures our love relationship. The gift of touch contains within it the miracle of healing and bonding. Touch is a means of connecting emotionally, physically and spiritually. The gentleness of touch communicates, "I love you." It can cause waves of tingles throughout your body and is not always a prelude to passion.

LoveNote. . . All there is, is relationships. Building a successful relationship is a never ending process. Work most on the first reality of your relationship - you. Your own personal growth contributes to the deepening and strengthening of the relationship you have with another. The second reality is your love partner. The relationship they have with themselves is only and always their responsibility. The third reality of a successful relationship is the 'us' of it. The joining of two whole people - complete in themselves - to do the work of a forever relationship is a worthy pursuit; one that is the most challenging and beautiful of all human experiences.

LoveNote... Your happiness can never come from someone else. It only comes from taking care of yourself, with feeling good about yourself and knowing that the time you invest in your own personal growth is one of the greatest contributions you can make to the relationship you have with your lover.

LoveNote. . . Choose to *be* in a relationship where the romance continues; where both partners continue to do things that you considered romantic when the relationship began.

LoveNote. . . It is possible to care without being a caretaker. We want our love partner to be happy. We want them to grow. We are very clear that it is not our responsibility to make sure this happens. We care. We are not obsessive and controlling about our caring. We let go of our attachment to the idea that we can make it happen *for* them. We let go of always trying to manipulate our way into taking over their problems, desires, needs and choices. We allow them to exercise responsible choices and be personally responsible for the consequences. We can care without caretaking.

LoveNote. . . In healthy love relationships we neither lead nor follow. We walk hand in hand, side by side. When it is appropriate, we can, without fear, let go for a while, always being nearby to love and to share. Love is no tug-of-war. We trust and respect our love partner giving them the freedom to be who they are, always with our love and best wishes.

RedHot LoveNote... If you want your sexual relationship to be enriched and enhanced, give your lover visual clues to sexual access. When you do, you give permission to your heart to explore the possibilities that love is. Flirt. Leave a sexy note on the bathroom mirror. Light some candles. Talk about making love. Whisper words that encourage fun in the bedroom and feel the passion mount. It can move mediocre sex to the level of fervent desire; the level necessary to have this special time together be awesome. It is okay to give yourselves something to look forward to.

LoveNote. . . Secret revelations about yourself to your love partner; the relevant truth - meaning revelations that relate to the love relationships' well being - make for intimate conversation that can assist a healthy love relationship to grow more passionate and deeply more intimate.

LoveNote. . . When relationships are fun they are easier to be appreciated. It takes steady work and a specific intention to have them be that way. It takes commitment, open communications and much love for one another. We must plan to have fun together. Playing and having fun together isn't so much what we do. It's how we feel about who we are with *and* what we do.

RedHot LoveNote. . . *Affirmation* ~ In the passion of making love, my love partner and I communicate a profundity of love that words cannot carry. Being together in this fully present and intimate way opens the channel of communication to allow for full disclosure of emotions and the expression of our innermost desires.

LoveNote. . . The commitment that supports a healthy partnership is the commitment each has to the other to always be working on the relationship; a commitment to always be in a dance with one another, showering each other with compassion and understanding.

LoveNote... Ask yourself: "Would I want to be in a relationship with me?" "Am I someone who I would want to be with forever?" Answer honestly. What comes up is always worth working on. Focus on doing what you can to make the good things better and give up behavior that has you curious enough to ask in the first place.

LoveNote. . . Tender moments of togetherness are necessary for a love relationship to grow. They must be tempered with the balance that the benefits of separateness also promote. The balance between closeness and separateness must be respected.

LoveNote... Intimate lovers don't have to say words to be understood. Often a knowing glance or touch can say all that needs to be said to ignite passion worthy of pursuit.

LoveNote. . . There is comfort in solitude. Love partners must learn to cherish their separateness while being together. A committed love relationship fosters respect; respect for each others' right to have some time to themselves.

LoveNote. . . Love is embracing differences and discovering ways in which to build a common lifestyle, share decision-making, and take equal responsibility for the results.

LoveNote... When you have disagreements, watch for the appropriate opportunity to share what is really in your heart. Little, if any progress can be made during meltdown. Allow a time for cooling off. This is a time when you must work together to create a space for each love partner to express their feelings without any fear that it isn't safe to do so. Listen. Communicate. Give up your attachment to being right and settle for a win/win solution that serves both love partners equally.

LoveNote. . . Trust creates breakthroughs in having relationships work. Among lovers, trust invites the spark of the Divine to ignite their passion. Trust keeps the magic of love alive.

LoveNote... A kiss has been described as the height of voluptuousness. It has a lovely, luscious and lusty legacy. Kissing is an act of quiet intimacy and often borders on the erotic. It can be brief and cool or lengthy and hot. It can be highly romantic, building to a succulent crescendo of emotion and passion or passed off as something that is expected and therefore no big deal. Two pairs of lips are for kissing. It is an essential element for communicating love and affection in your relationship. A kiss speaks many different meanings to its lover; when it is missing, many interpretations as to the reasons for its absence surface. These interpretations can become invisible wedges that prevent love from expressing. When love is present, kissing is an important part of expressing that love. Pay attention to it. Kissing does not always have to be a prelude to making love.

LoveNote. . . *Affirmation* ~ I am learning to be conscious when I am with my love partner. Many times in the past, I only appeared to be listening. Now I listen. I am conscious of, pay attention to and really listen, with genuine interest, to my lover; my best friend. This new attitude of attention and understanding gives our relationship substance. It gives it depth. It becomes charged with right intention.

LoveNote. . . When you are in a relationship with someone and both of you are angry, chaos abounds. Two broken people can't fix each other! They can only work on the problem. "What is the problem," you ask? The answer is looking back at you in the mirror. Recovery comes from ceasing to be one of the problems.

LoveNote. . . People who love each other learn to respect their inherent differences. Men and women think, feel and communicate differently. Understanding this is the key. With understanding comes acceptance. With acceptance comes the ultimate expression of unconditional love.

LoveNote. . . There is power in a hug. Hugs bring people together. This expression of human touch can silently speak forgiveness, sensitivity, acceptance, caring, healing and love.

LoveNote. . . Love is something you do. Love is as love does. Never be content with only telling your love partner you love them; promise to show it in expressions of affection. Plan to be spontaneously affectionate.

LoveNote. . . Committed love partners know it is wise to plan their time together. Go on a date. Talk about it. Plan it in advance. Don't wait until the last moment. Take turns planning these events. Lovers show their consideration for each other this way. To do otherwise is to take your togetherness for granted.

LoveNote. . . *Affirmation* ~ I have a relationship that is a self-sustaining vehicle for personal and spiritual growth; one that supports and encourages a positive climate for consistent change; one that offers patience, understanding and forgiveness when errors are made.

LoveNote. . . Feelings are always very real for the one who feels them. When your lover expresses feelings. . . validate them. Let them know that it is okay to feel that way, even when you disagree. When you invalidate your love partner's feelings, generally disagreement follows. Never argue with anyone's feelings. It's an argument you can never win.

LoveNote. . . Disagreements are a signal that your love partner needs care and understanding. Develop a way of listening that allows you to hear the anger without becoming defensive. Because they are angry does not mean you are not loved. You can love and be angry at the same time.

LoveNote. . . *For Men Only* ~ It is difficult to understand and correctly interpret what someone is feeling when no one is talking. This is often a great challenge for women when suddenly their man shuts down and ceases to communicate. This strategy seldom works for the good of the relationship. Women usually communicate their feelings with words. It is wise for a man to learn that to be understood; silence is not golden. With communicated agreements about how and when you can express yourself, and an understanding between love partners about listening without contradiction, being vulnerable becomes easier. When love is present in your relationship, it is easier to risk saying what you need to say. Words, carefully chosen, spoken aloud, are the only way for a woman to know what is in your heart. Learning to express yourself aloud is one thing, the feelings behind how you express these words are what counts. Your love partner must feel the love behind the words.

LoveNote. . . Pain is a given. Suffering is optional. Those things that hurt, instruct. Love becomes a deeper experience of unity amid diversity. A commitment to work together rather than run from the problem requires a willingness to risk being hurt and rejected, and yes, at times, even feeling un-loved.

LoveNote... Rarely does anyone get what they need from a relationship when their only intention is to criticize their lover for mistakes or to offer assistance that is not asked for.

LoveNote. . . When misunderstandings surface, it is easy to misinterpret what is really going on. Remember that how you express your anger is being translated by someone who has no idea how *you* feel. It is as if love partners speak two different languages. It is often difficult to remember this when you are in the heat of battle. Wait for the dust to settle, then ask your lover to translate their feelings in a way that you can listen. . . with understanding.

LoveNote... There can be no intimacy without conversation. The only way you and your love partner can truly communicate is to tell the truth about how you feel. Truthful communication moves love partners closer together; it creates a condition of unity, love and satisfaction.

LoveNote. . . *For Women Only* ~ When your lover needs space. . . allow it. When he pulls away. . . *let him go.* He will be back. Remember, to pursue him or to punish him when this happens will only continue to interrupt the intimacy you both so fervently desire.

LoveNote... Use your mistakes as avenues through which you can expand your awareness, knowledge and understanding. Many relationship difficulties are born out of a lack of understanding.

LoveNote. . . *For Men Only* ~ When your lover is hurting and tells you so, this is not a request for "Mr. Fix-it." First, she is not broken. Second, always remember, someone who is hurting only needs your love, support and understanding. A warm and tender hug might help. Whisper that you understand and in your best way, let her know she is loved.

LoveNote... Open and intimate conversation is the only way you can avoid the mistake of only giving what you would like to receive instead of giving what your love partner really needs. Negotiate for what you both want and need and respect the differences.

LoveNote. . . *For Men Only* ~ It's okay to say you are sorry. Saying you are sorry doesn't always mean you did anything wrong. When your lover is experiencing difficulties, "I'm sorry" can be an expression of understanding; it demonstrates an attitude of caring and empathy.

LoveNote. . . Things change. Feelings change. Needs change. Wants change. In a healthy love relationship you must remember to communicate these changes in a loving way as they occur. How sad to change your feelings in a positive way and never communicate them to your love partner. Effective communication is required. It cannot happen by osmosis.

LoveNote. . . When you are not receiving the support you feel you need, it may be necessary to ask for it. Indirect requests seldom, if ever, work. Non-specific requests often cause feelings of being taken for granted. Be clear about the kind of support you need and present your request by asking directly.

LoveNote. . . *Affirmation For Men Only* ~ I am open to share my innermost secret thoughts and feelings with her. Being open and getting to know and be known by my lover is exciting and emotionally enriching.

RedHot LoveNote. . . The intimate and trusting atmosphere two lovers create together when making love allows for an occasional flirting with mutually acceptable fantasies; a powerful stimulus to sexual pleasure. Anything goes as long as love prevails; touch, tongue, tickle; silk, satin, lace; the kitchen table, the patio in the moonlight, the hot tub or Bennigan's parking lot!

LoveNote... Mature love partners permit each other the freedom to pursue their individual interests and friends without restriction. This is when trust presents itself. Mature love allows this level of separateness to bring lovers closer together. In this scenario separateness is perceived as a bond... not a wedge. It encourages love partners to celebrate their own uniqueness.

LoveNote. . . How wonderful to be in a relationship where love partners feel free to express their wants and needs. It is a healthy relationship where love partners can ask for what they want from each other and feel the freedom to say yes or no without feeling that they 'should' respond in any particular way. Learn to be okay with the answer you get. Rejection and disapproval are not in the vocabulary of lovers who are in a healthy love relationship.

LoveNote... For intimacy to grow in a healthy love relationship there can be no withholding. Feelings - the relevant truth - both positive and negative, must be shared equally between love partners... in a loving way.

LoveNote... *Affirmation For Men Only* ~ I want the best for my love partner and will never feel threatened by her successes in any way. My love partner is unique and I love her for who she is, not for what I may expect her to be. I encourage emotional self-sufficiency in my love partner. I believe that the need for individual autonomy is not only compatible with a successful forever relationship, but can only be a strong contributor.

LoveNote. . . Manage your relationship in a way that has both of you have fun in it. Having fun together must be one of your highest priorities.

LoveNote. . . When we disagree, our relationship can often become 'temporarily out of order.' Arguments that bring anger to the boiling point are most destructive. Restoration is a process. It requires patience, understanding, acceptance and much love. Discuss with an intention to resolve the conflict. Give up being right. Arguments create negative distance. We must move through conflict as quickly as we can. Life is too short to maintain negative distance between love partners for lengthy periods of time.

LoveNote. . . You do not stumble on a great relationship by accident. You experience it on purpose. It doesn't just happen. A great relationship is developed intentionally. It is created by mutual commitment and by nurturing it with loving thoughts, open communication, the attention given to it, intentional activity and a mutual decision for constructive action. It becomes whatever two love partners decide it to be. It is the result of two dancing hearts being in step with one another; dancing to the same rhythm; connected; communicating words of love in a dance of togetherness.

LoveNote. . . *For Singles Only* ~ The heart is crying for adventure, which can only be found by embarking on your own personal journey of self-discovery. You will discover your sense of adventure in a state of solitude, not in a relationship. Your sense of adventure will carry over into the relationship, but can never genuinely be found there to begin with. You create your own sense of adventure. Your heart may never be free enough to really be adventurous until, at your new level of awareness, you recognize the value of love-of-self. Within this very personal accomplishment you will discover the richest source of self-esteem and unconditional love. Then comes the adventure!

LoveNote... When we are angry our feelings change from moment to moment. Anger produces feelings that are unreliable. Our feelings often rise and fall as our energy is drawn from the unstable emotions present when anger is being expressed. In those moments our feelings may not be the most reliable source of information to help us move past it. Before you blow up, cool down.

LoveNote. . . Plateaus and setbacks are natural to progress. Growth in an intimate relationship is never in a straight, upward line.

RedHot LoveNote. . . The sexual experience is immeasurably heightened when both love partners feel free to mutually share their likes and dislikes, cares and concerns and honor each other for their choices.

LoveNote. . . The goal of resolving conflict in a relationship is not victory or defeat. It is reaching a mutual understanding through open discussions that benefits both love partners. It requires letting go of our need to be right. Mutually solving problems brings love partners closer together. It allows for negotiation and compromise. It promotes positive momentum.

LoveNote. . . *Affirmation* ~ When I allow my love partner to see me for who I really am right now, I am less afraid I will be rejected in the future.

LoveNote... It is the mistaken belief that you must push your love relationship in the direction you think it should go that keeps you in a strained and unhappy relationship with it. Reality has its own effortless course, and you can either embrace its way or struggle endlessly with your way.

LoveNote. . . A determination to resolve conflict by conversation offers a chance for healing and promotes the opportunity to become closer to the one you love. Cherish your differences. They are there for a purpose. Learn from them by learning to freely discuss them. Withhold your disapproval. Listen with acceptance and understanding. Conversation occurs when someone is speaking and someone is listening. Being an attentive listener often offers an opportunity for healing and suggests a deeper level of love than simply saying, "I love you!"

LoveNote. . . *For Singles Only* ~ The relationship of your heart's desire will manifest itself when you, in earnest, consistently do everything you can to make it happen. Doing what you can to make it happen means taking care of yourself. It means being okay with being alone; loving your own company. When you reach this level of awareness, your true love will sneak up on you. Be careful not to make the mistake of looking for a relationship. That only keeps it away.

LoveNote. . . In a sense, a great love relationship lives on the tip of your tongue. Things go well because you *both* say so. . . and because of what each of you do. The thoughts you have about yourself, your love partner and your love relationship often end up in the words you speak in your relationship. Words can never be recalled. Once out there. . . they do their intended work; interpreted however they may be by your love partner. The words you speak determine what shows up in your relationship. Relationships cannot be truly great and utterly incredible unless you make internal changes in the way you think and take caution of the words you speak.

LoveNote. . . *Affirmation For Men Only* ~ I always remember that more often than not, when my love partner wants to talk, she only wants someone to listen and not to dispense advice.

LoveNote... An exciting, adventurous relationship only happens when you become exciting and adventurous! With excitement and adventure present in your love relationship, you will never have to re-ignite the flame of love... only keep it burning.

RedHot LoveNote. . . Foreplay is often found in the quietness of loving words.

LoveNote. . . *For Singles Only* ~ You must be content to first be happy alone so you can be happy when you are together with someone else. Happy and healthy relationships are usually made between happy and healthy people; people who were happy and healthy before they became love partners.

LoveNote... Healthy, committed love partners will say, "I'm sorry. I was wrong," and mean it, rather than hold on to being right or walking away.

LoveNote. . . Love is the answer. Genuine unconditional love is the kind of love you know is there
even when it doesn't feel like it; the kind that has no
preconceived notions or undelivered communications. It always delivers on its promise. It's the kind
of love that you can stand on and know it will never
let you down.

LoveNote. . . *Affirmation* ~ The greatest rewards of living and loving come when I step out of the bounds of my ordinary existence and extend myself beyond what I believe my limits to be. I am willing to give myself to the relationship without giving myself up in the relationship, and to be willing to be what grows out of it.

LoveNote. . . Starting over is the key to a new you. Embrace the beauty and significance of starting over - over and over and over. Every present moment is always new and new is always right now! The new dies to the ever-new in an endless celebration of love of Life. This is it! Right now is the only reality.

LoveNote. . . Become a happiness enhancer. You can never make someone else happy. That is only and always their choice. You can, however, do things that enhance the happiness others experience. Dream up a few happy and healthy ways to *be* that will turn your lover on to happiness. This calls for being creative with your thoughtfulness, being playfully attentive and caring enough to say, "I love you" for no other reason than you experience happiness when you express love in this random and thoughtful way.

LoveNote. . . Intimacy is the only path to passion. Not sharing intimately negates the opportunity to grow together. Honesty in communication bonds two lovers in a very special way. A lack of open communication closes the door to intimacy, passion, great sex and unconditional love. Dare to reveal yourself. Become transparent, not invisible. . . transparent. Let your lover see through you to the real you. The depth of connection that comes from genuine intimacy is unimaginable and worth it!

LoveNote. . . Be challenged by engaging in meaningful conversation. Talk about things that are important to your relationship. Don't leave anything out. Develop a relationship that creates the freedom to talk about what needs to be said, without arguments. . . only conversations. It's not easy. It takes giving your love partner the freedom to speak what is in his or her heart. It takes knowing that what they speak about is only their opinion, they have a right to it and are responsible for it. The challenge is to be okay with that.

LoveNote. . . *Affirmation* ~ My partner and I take turns creating an adventure day or weekend outing that is memorable and exciting for both of us. We look for creative ways to have fun to keep the magic of love alive. We are committed to use our imagination and enjoy one another. We pledge to have fun doing whatever it takes.

LoveNote. . . There can be no unconditional love without trust. Arms length trust does not work. Withholding trust creates a barrier around your heart. A relationship without trust is guarded. . . it is tainted by a lack of full self-expression with the one you love.

RedHot LoveNote. . . Experiencing the unknown is one of the best ways to add some excitement to the sexual part of your relationship. Experiment in the bedroom. Be challenged to discover the immense stimulation that comes from really *being* together. . . holding, touching, kissing. Do what comes naturally. Never be wedded to any set ideas of how making love 'should' be. Let go. Variety *is* the spice of your sexual life. Be open to whatever happens. Make love with the idea that orgasm, when it comes, will be the bonus. Foreplay as a shared adventure creates a mutually appreciated and loving bond between lovers.

LoveNote. . . *For Singles Only* ~ The same energy we use to hold on to the past is the same energy we need to create our future. The extent to which we cling to the past is the extent to which we are blocked in receiving what we truly want in a future relationship.

LoveNote. . . Often we are not present in our relationship. We are either looking into the past with regret or into the future with concern. This is it! To experience the reality of the present we must learn to live *in the present;* to be present to the experience of right now. The possibilities of the present are only available to those who are willing to live and love *in the present.* We cannot change the past and a concern for the future allows us to be absent from the present. Both options keep us stuck! Live and love every moment of right now!

LoveNote. . . *For Men Only* ~ A woman wants to be respected as a woman, not as your wife or, heaven forbid, your mother!

LoveNote. . . True love allows for disagreements. Acknowledging when you are wrong is not a sign of weakness; it is a sign of strength.

LoveNote. . . *For Singles Only* ~ Make having a great relationship with yourself your number one priority. Spend time working on you. It is a prerequisite to having a healthy love relationship with someone else. Work on developing your own self as an individual. Reinvent a relationship with yourself. Make it a new and exciting relationship; one you can be proud to carry over into your next relationship with someone else. Allow a time for healing the hurts of the past. Nobody wants damaged goods.

LoveNote... The energy we give to our troubles by dwelling on them, saps us of the energy we need to find solutions for them. They seem to linger longer the more we pay attention to them. Troubles feed on the energy we give them. Troubles deny us the opportunity that lies just past them. Never ask why troubles come. Be grateful there are solutions. We need to redirect our energy. This deflates the ego of troubles. Focus on the promise of a better tomorrow by acknowledging our troubles, then immediately get busy working on the discovery of workable solutions. If we are to choose to make things work, we need to listen for answers. We cannot do this when we are immersed in the turmoil of confusion. It takes much energy to remain confused.

LoveNote. . . *Affirmation* ~ When I am hurting, I ask my lover for a hug. There is Divine healing in a silent, close embrace.

Larry James

LoveNote... If you ever reach a point in your relationship where you think you have nothing good to say about your love partner, close your mouth until you think of something good to say... then say it. You tell yourself what to think... tell yourself to 'shut up' when the temptation to speak ill of your lover occurs.

LoveNote. . . Two love partners, standing firm - together - can accomplish anything the two of them desire. The creative movement of mutual commitment can produce anything. . . joy, peace of mind, more love, great sex, understanding. . . anything! The unity of two, in agreement, does the work of angels.

LoveNote. . . Trust demands no withholds. It invites personal disclosure. When you trust the one you're with, you can step in front of the person you've been, allow your lover to see the real you and be more of your true self. You can more lovingly express how you think and feel when trust is present and feel more free to do so.

LoveNote. . . *Affirmation* ~ For me to experience the kind of relationship I want, I accept that to understand each other, my love partner and I must have clearly developed channels of communication.

LoveNote. . . A healthy love relationship is a safe place where two lovers can be themselves. No more pretending. It's almost as if both spirits merge. It's about experiencing the freedom to be real and about feeling okay about ourselves and the relationship. No more judgments or preconceived notions of how it 'should' be. It's about each giving consent to be loved and appreciated for who they are and loving each other for having the courage to be that way.

LoveNote... Change is always possible in our relationship because it is only and always a choice. Taking responsibility for our choices leads to a profound sense of freedom and inner peace.

LoveNote... In reality, anger is a derivative of and an expression of fear. To transcend or master fear, we must turn our back on it; exercise courage. Love cannot exist in the presence of fear. It is impossible for opposites to co-exist. They cannot occupy the same space at the same time. So... we drift. Back and forth. Love. Fear. Love. Fear. We must learn to express love to ourselves and to others in the midst of upsets. Releasing anger in healthy ways proves we are capable of creative acts of wholeness. Healing is always around the corner. It shows up when we have the courage to let go of the anger and fully embrace love.

LoveNote... Indifference is like water to a fire. The flame of love grows dim with indifference to your love partner's needs.

LoveNote. . . *For Singles Only* ~ If you do not cherish the companionship you find with yourself then you can never find it with someone else. It is important to be your own best friend. Doing so gives you knowledge of yourself. You must have a clear understanding of what true friendship is before you can earn the right to share it with someone else. Once that status is achieved, the warmth of the friendship you have for yourself will radiate and attract another who has shared a similar experience; someone who will appreciate you for the true friend you really are.

LoveNote. . . Trust introduces you to a new freedom - the freedom to think and feel and really *be*
with the one you love. Trust opens the door to un-
limited possibilities.

LoveNote... Anger spills over into all areas of your life. Unresolved anger transfers to others you are in relationship with. Anger, when released, without dumping on your relationship, is good. Anger is not bad. We only call it bad because we feel its negative energy. It is only bad when we express it in hurtful and thoughtless ways.

LoveNote... *Affirmation* ~ I resist having expectations for what I think my love partner *should* do for me. Ours is a love relationship without 'shoulds;' a relationship of individual choice; one of celebration of our right to choose individually while playing full-out as a team.

LoveNote. . . Men and women often perceive the same situation differently. They both are watching the same picture but to one, the picture may be blurred and out of focus. To the other, everything is crystal clear. There are as many opinions about things as there are people. Not everyone is on the same frequency. When you do the work of healthy love relationships, you are always about the business of fine-tuning your relationship so that when different versions of the same picture show up, you can lovingly communicate your different perceptions and love each other for having shared them in a healthy way.

LoveNote. . . Heart-to-heart communication requires an emotional atmosphere of caring, safety, and trust. A healthy love relationship allows two people to fully know each other and still love each other.

LoveNote... Resist being afraid to reveal your limitations to your partner. Yes, it's scary, and you are now a team. Your partner will almost always be the most dependable, the first in line to care, and the first to help, if help is requested. Often all that is needed is someone who will listen. First, it is okay to make yourself vulnerable. Next, working together on strengthening limitations develops character. It promotes unity by creating a common bond of sharing that helps each other be the best they can be for themselves and for the relationship.

LoveNote. . . You cannot change someone else. It simply is not possible. Give it up. Love them and work on you. Never stop working on you. If your love partner doesn't keep up, who fault is that? It's a sad state of affairs, but you have to live with 'you' for the rest of your life. You are the most important person in the relationship. You come first. Change yourself and you give others the power to change if they choose to. Being the best you can be in spite of your partner's lack of interest in personal growth or the growth of the relationship can be the very thing that serves as the inspiration needed for them to be willing to initiate change for themselves.

LoveNote. . . Trust brings lovers together. Consider it a Divine joining; the inevitable interweaving that occurs when two people love unconditionally and become as one. A feeling of deep inner security comes from the trust that is present with unconditional love; a love that never needs to be negotiated.

LoveNote. . . We often cannot see that we have choice. No matter what happens we *always* have choice. The hurt we experience sometimes keeps us at a distance from responsible choices. We can move through the pain of a changing relationship much more rapidly when we remember that we are never without choice.

LoveNote. . . *Affirmation For Men Only* ~ I cultivate transparency of myself by being a master in the art of self-disclosure. I know that when the inclination to reveal myself to the one I love is blocked, I close myself to her and experience emotional difficulties. I promise to never hide behind a facade.

LoveNote. . . An essential part of true listening is the discipline of temporarily giving up or setting aside your own prejudices, frames of reference and desires to experience as much as possible your love partner's world from the inside; hearing what is truly from the heart.

LoveNote. . . *For Singles Only* ~ Letting go is not complicated. It is simple. Not easy. Simply identify the situation you want to let go of and ask yourself, "Am I willing to waste my energy further on this matter?" If the answer is "no," then that's it! Let go. Telling someone is a bonus. Detachment is only for you, never for another. It promotes healing. Choice is always present when you let go. You do not have to let go *and* there are consequences.

LoveNote. . . It is never appropriate to suppress anger or to disregard how we really feel about it. When we feel anger, it is a very real feeling; at that moment, we have an intimate relationship with it. Anger is difficult to contain. When we are angry, we often feel a need to demonstrate it, talk about it and let people know that we are indeed angry. Only and always talking about it is not enough. Talking about it helps only if your intention is to seek to understand it or to find a way through it, not to justify it or hold on to it.

LoveNote... *Affirmation* ~ My love partner and I share similar spiritual values. Higher spiritual values give meaning and purpose to our relationship. They determine what we will turn away from and what we will move toward. Shared spiritual ideas are the basis for a lasting, fulfilling love relationship.

LoveNote. . . When two lovers have been together for a long time, passion can often be dampened by the comfort of shared routines and especially muted by daily activities when they are apart. To enjoy a more satisfying level of intimacy, spend time working to recapture the excitement of your best times together. Take time-out for the two of you; a special time, free of all distractions, to indulge in reminiscence. Develop a plan to add festivity, playfulness and romantic happenings to the times you spend with one another. From this shared activity, you will experience a higher level of compassion for each other and the reassurance of forever love that may have been missing. Good fortune favors those who actively work together to create a sense of shared responsibility for the success of their relationship.

LoveNote. . . *Affirmation* ~ In a healthy love relationship there is always movement, at first toward intimacy, at other times toward withdrawal and distance. I am secure in my love relationship and never panic during a difficult phase of withdrawal. I unconditionally love my partner and remember my commitment to do whatever it takes to encourage the experience of balance in our love relationship.

RedHot LoveNote... Be aware of and from time to time relive those special moments of shared intimacy in private conversations. Pledge to keep alive the simple pleasures that keep the fire burning for both of you. Plan to have fun in the bedroom together. The couple that plays together... stays together.

LoveNote. . . Intentionally add a little pizzazz to your love relationship every day. Do it in playful ways. Exercise your sense of humor. It enlivens your spirit, breeds happiness and causes you and the one you love to experience fully the love you feel for one another. Do things that make each other smile. Smiles and knowing nods from your lover create a sense of unity that adds longevity to your relationship.

LoveNote. . . *Affirmation For Women Only* ~ I always allow my love partner to be his own separate person. The object is not to be as one. It is to trust each other enough to be their own person and play together as a team. A healthy love relationship can exist only between two strong and independent people.

LoveNote. . . We often get so busy working on trying to fix our love partner - an impossible task, I might add - that we forget that we are responsible for only fixing ourselves.

LoveNote... To have found someone you can share your love and life with is one of life's greatest treasures and most exciting adventures.

LoveNote... Growing older together is but another stage of growing up together. Assisting one another in this process allows for a growing together that can only be experienced by a mutually specific intention. Helping one another is at the heart of a lasting friendship. It is the kind of loving guidance that will sustain you in any situation. Looking back you will be able to serenely celebrate the love and support that brought you to the present and know the best is yet to be!

LoveNote. . . *For Women Only* ~ Men tend to grow at their own speed. Unless your love partner is intentional about personal growth, anything you say to help may only cause him to feel that you think he is broken. Right or wrong, men inherently believe they can handle their own stuff. This may or may not be true, but being insistent about helping him grow can temporarily shut him out of your life. Quit trying to fix him. Be there for him when he is ready to be cared for, otherwise let him be and quietly attend to yourself.

LoveNote... If you want an adventurous heart experience in which the thirst for love is quenched forever by a love relationship blessed with unconditional love... *trust is the only answer.*

LoveNote... When partners really love each other; when two hearts leap together in unison, we can expect to experience an indescribable sense of exuberance that only two lovers can create. Each moment together becomes a moment of sheer joy; moments we will treasure forever. Forever lovers. Two dancing hearts conveying mutual respect; a symbol of the closeness we share. . . a cherished togetherness; each lover always doing their best to be in step in a dance of unconditional love. Neither will ever have to say, "Are we there yet?"

LoveNote... *Affirmation* ~ If I feel my lover taking me for granted, it is always and only my responsibility to request the love and appreciation I deserve.

LoveNote. . . Promise to always openly communicate affection and commitment. It gives your future together more of a chance. Put aside any hesitancy to display affection at times other than when you want something.

LoveNote... The psychological importance of working through painful resentments must not be underestimated. When old patterns are broken, a whole new world of possibility is born. Not to release and rise above suppressed feelings of hurt and anger is to remain imprisoned by them.

LoveNote... To have an intimate love relationship, love partners need to feel the freedom to live their lives together in ways that satisfy each of them individually and still meet each others needs.

LoveNote. . . Love and miracles go hand in hand. They are synonymous. Where you find one, you will always find the other. If you want more miracles in your love relationship, express more love. Never take love or miracles for granted. When you do, they go away.

LoveNote... *For Women Only* ~ When you feel your love partner lagging behind in the relationship, it is often difficult to back away from what seems to be a responsibility to assist him. Smothering your lover with attempts to help can give the appearance that you think he is unable to make his own responsible choices. No one can change anything without the freedom to do so. Smothering feels like 'no freedom' to a man. Your energy will soon be depleted if your love partner has little desire to change. Nurture him with your love and support. Be there when he needs someone to listen. Only offer help when it is requested.

LoveNote. . . *For Singles Only* ~ It's simple. Not easy. The path to a whole and healthy love relationship begins when you self-inquire; it begins with loving you. Look at what you've been doing. If it isn't working, give up being right about it and change it! Now!

LoveNote. . . Forgive and forget is an impossibility. Forgive? Yes! You forgive because it sets you free; the first step toward healing. Forget? No! You always remember. Keep your word. Trust is a fragile issue. A breach of trust is never forgotten. Be careful of the words you speak in your relationship. They cannot be taken back. Each word will be burned into the memory of your love partner. Think before you speak. Words create. They either build up or tear down. Speak only words of love. Words can come back to haunt you or they can become the way two lovers express sensitivity, warmth, understanding, acceptance and love.

LoveNote... *Affirmation* ~ I see upsets in my relationship not only as an exterior circumstance to be remedied, but as an interior condition to be understood and healed.

LoveNote. . . Trust blazes new trails. It creates the opening for intimacy to exist. It opens up new opportunities to really *be* with the one you love. Love can eliminate the fear of trusting, for fear cannot exist in the presence of love. Among lovers, trust invites the spark of the Divine to ignite their passion. When trust is present in a love relationship you will find two hearts dancing. . . another true miracle of love.

LoveNote. . . It is always possible for you to direct the energy of anger in another completely different direction, even though it may not seem so at the time. The same energy you expend on anger, when redirected, can be put to use in a much more useful direction. Think about it. If you choose to shorten your attention span on what makes you angry, you can immediately put that same energy to use by focusing on the solution to the upset that caused the anger in the first place.

LoveNote. . . Insecurities bring forth jealousy, which, is a cry for more love. It is within your rights to ask for more affection when self-doubts surface, however, the indirect way that jealousy asks for it is counterproductive. Excessive possessiveness is inappropriate. Jealousy is the surest way to drive away the very person you may fear losing.

LoveNote... *Affirmation* ~ I know that if I want my love relationship to fulfill its purpose, I must enlighten my experience of it. I must drop judgments, pre-conceived notions, opinions, expectations, positions and beliefs about it. When I do this, a miracle occurs. The miracle that occurs is that the love relationship I have becomes the love relationship I want; the one that nurtures and supports me; the one that truly empowers my love partner and me.

LoveNote. . . When self-discovery becomes more important than being right, then every situation in our relationship will present us with an opportunity to learn about ourselves in a new and exciting way.

LoveNote. . . You are the architect of your own discomfort. The secret is to never wallow in the suffering any longer than is necessary to learn the lesson the suffering presents.

LoveNote. . . The fire of love will not burn on alone. It must be watched carefully. If we are to keep the fire of love alive, we must do whatever is necessary to keep the fuel for the flames replenished whatever the cost. Loves' fire feeds off the energy we put into keeping it burning!

RedHot LoveNote. . . *Affirmation* ~ A balance of excitement and quiet pleasures allows a relationship to maximize its potential. My love partner and I have a deep need for the gentleness of a passionate kiss, tenderness, caressing, fondling, and touching each other.

LoveNote... Forgiveness is for *your* benefit. It gives *you* the freedom to move forward. Telling someone you forgive them is a bonus *and* it is not necessary for forgiveness to be complete. Forgiveness will release you from all personal suffering and feelings of loss. Forgiveness is a mental attitude. Once convinced of its own idea, forgiveness is complete; freedom follows.

LoveNote... If you don't set relationship goals, you will always be wondering what tomorrow holds. When you get sick and tired of that, you will do something different. Most likely, not before.

LoveNote. . . Working together in a love relationship to get your individual needs met and the mutual needs of the relationship and *not have expectations about how those needs get met* will always generate new things to talk about. Having expectations about how your needs get met is not only unrealistic it is an unhealthy attitude. For example, if I *expect* you to love me a certain way and your love doesn't show up that way for me, I will most likely be disappointed. A better way might be to have your need for being loved fulfilled by allowing your love partner to love you the way *they* love you. Being okay with how they love you creates a sense of adventure; it creates new and exciting possibilities for the two of you to experience together. Often challenges show up. However, when two people really love each other and are committed to work together, challenges like these create the kind of conversation that empowers both love partners to continue to self-inquire. They then choose to investigate their curiosities about what they can do to stand together, to be challenged by this new way of being and know that everything is going to be okay.

LoveNote. . . *Affirmation* ~ I am learning how to overcome my limitations and develop my capacity to love, not because I expect love in return, but simply because my love partner deserves to be loved.

LoveNote. . . Making love is a Divine idea!

LoveNote. . . In *healthy* love relationships, there is no second place. There is no longer any need to have one of you be number one and one of you be number two. *Healthy people share.* In a healthy love relationship, generosity expresses itself generously. Love partners are not afraid to share the spotlight. Give up the idea of having to have any one of the two people who make up a relationship be subservient. When two people really love each other, they are not afraid to be their love partner's equal. Two people, each number one to each other *and* to the relationship, working together on similar things and accepting mutual responsibility when things are good and also when things are not so good, can only empower the relationship. You give *of* yourself to the other. You never give up yourself *to* the other. When you are both number one, no one ever has to worry about competition in the relationship. When two people work together, they can always accomplish more.

LoveNote. . . Anger hurts most whoever is angry. Choosing to be angry is choosing to suffer. Suffering is always optional. Only express your anger to get it out, not to win. In a healthy love relationship, expressions of anger are always followed by expressions of love.

LoveNote. . . There is no victory without the willingness to risk setbacks or total defeat. Neither is there any conquest of unconditional love in a relationship without the sacred bond that comes from a total commitment to team. Unconditional love implies commitment and the mature exercise of wisdom.

LoveNote... A great relationship begins with you. Make yourself better than you ever thought you could be and you will find the relationship you have with your love partner getting better. This works especially well when two people are focusing on working on themselves; together. Then, the relationship you have with the one you love can only grow and prosper. Only selfish people think only of themselves. When you really love yourself you cannot help wanting to give some of your love away. Other people have a need to be loved. So do you. People are like that. Like attracts like. What you become you attract. Want a great love partner? Become a great love partner! Work on this one. Sharing love with someone else must only and always begin with you. Learn to relate to yourself better.

LoveNote. . . The energy required for the self-discipline of honesty is far less than the energy required for withholding what is in your heart. Withholding is always a matter of integrity. It is always potentially a lie. The cause of withholding is fear. Love is the answer. Fear cannot exist in the presence of Love.

LoveNote. . . Relationship problems do not go away. They must be worked through or else they remain, forever a barrier to the growth and development of the human spirit. Trials and tribulations are to make, not break us.

LoveNote. . . Mature love partners have learned not to expect perfection in each other. They know that acceptance has its own reward. Each lover's differences test the other's capacity for acceptance, forgiveness and understanding. They never dance around issues. When necessary, they discuss their imperfections, lovingly, with care not to pass judgment with harmful words. Acceptance and tolerance hold hands in the presence of unconditional love.

LoveNote. . . Only one thing activates, then converts the negative energy of anger into positive energy. . . *intention.* The intention must be to do something different; something that works. When you discover that what you have been doing isn't working, the only logical thing to do is to do something different. We are talking about change. Yes, it is uncomfortable to change. You must decide which is the most uncomfortable. The same energy you expend on anger, when re-directed, can help free you of the negative emotions you feel when you are angry. Freeing yourself of these negative emotions is something *you* do. It is never dependent upon whoever or whatever you think is the cause of your anger.

LoveNote... A constructive argument; one that does not seek to make your love partner wrong and make you right; one that searches for understanding; one that releases tension and facilitates an emotionally healthy breakthrough, can help your relationship evolve to a new level of love and understanding.

LoveNote. . . *For Singles Only* ~ Beware of dancing hormones! They often mask a multitude of stuff. You know what I mean. It's that time when both of your antennas go up! You're tuned in to each other. Your body tells you things you didn't know about yourself. Your heart is dancing! Is it your heart or your hormones? To some, that is the fun part; a time for romance; the time when you are deep in thought. . . "Is this the one?" While it's true that this part of a relationship feels good, perhaps you should follow your heart instead of your hormones on this one. The hormones will scream words like: 'forget all that stuff about healthy love relationships, live fast, love hard and get this one before he or she gets away!' or 'carve another notch, this one's the same as in bed!' or whatever the hormones moan. Your heart will whisper words like: 'take it easy!' - 'one step at a time!' - 'get to know each other' - 'tell each other the relevant truth' - 'make sure it's love and not just sex!' or whatever the heart could say that would be words of love and encouragement. Only and always listen to your heart!

LoveNote. . . As we come to understand our equal share in creating problems. . . blame, self-doubt, and discord gives way to personal responsibility, accountability, mutual respect and intimacy. In a healthy love relationship, things are easiest when both love partners take responsibility for the whole, not just their halves.

LoveNote. . . Trust commands that you live in the present, trusting one moment at a time. To fully trust takes time and mature, committed love.

RedHot LoveNote. . . Learn to share your passion with your lover without fear. Share it with patience, commitment, and trust. This level of emotional sharing generates a limitless flow of sexual energy. Seek not just sensory gratification but Divine union with your love partner.

LoveNote. . . *Affirmation* ~ I have a love partner who is supportive of us making key choices together, fully listening to and learning from what each love partner has to say.

LoveNote. . . Isn't it interesting? We have good intentions, yet, somehow we often never seem to get around to doing everything we know must be done to stimulate healthy love relationships. 'Green lights and straight ahead' sounds like a great idea! Good intentions without affirmative action get you nowhere. Our intentions are good and we take left turns. We intend to be on the right path and we get distracted or we don't have time. Or, "If he or she would only change!" Or, anything to keep from taking responsibility for the direction we really want to go in the relationship. Stay on the path. Avoid all distractions. Focus. It is stupid not to do something different, when what you are doing isn't working! Relationships are worth any price it takes to have them. Not in the sense of doing *anything* to have a relationship, but in the sense of each of you always doing the best you can, all the time, to have the relationship be good and healthy. It doesn't get any better than that!

LoveNote... Courage. It takes courage! To have a healthy love relationship you must take a leap of faith. The faith is in the leap; the leap into the unknown. In that moment you decide. With all the love you possess as your support, you make the decision for change in the presence of fear. In doing so, fear goes away. The miracle of the adventure lies in living life in the leap! Two hearts - committed to be true to the other - will carry one another safely to the other side.

LoveNote. . . Intimacy, the most profound of inter-personal human pleasures, grows most favorably in an atmosphere of peace and love.

LoveNote. . . We often expect our love partner to make the best choices for themselves and our relationship and when they are not *our* choices, we often get angry or disappointed. . . or both. Most people call this situation a problem; a problem we create by our expectations. Try this: 'no expectations, fewer disappointments.' It's that simple. Not easy. Simple. No expectations equal unconditional love. We all experience the need to have healthy choices exercised and when they don't show up, we either choose to have conversations about them or not. If the choices are abusive and therefore unacceptable, we begin to think about making a responsible choice to leave the relationship. However, always picking our lover apart because their choices are not the ones we would make can only point the relationship in the direction of failure. If we could accept the notion that everyone is doing the best they can, regardless of whether their choices are our choices, our attitude about our relationship would improve and perhaps the relationship we have would become the relationship we enjoy being in.

LoveNote. . . *For Men Only* ~ By far the most common and important way in which you can exercise your attention to your love partner is by listening. Listening is an act of love. It is unreasonable, and a breach of trust, to deny your lover's report of her feelings.

LoveNote. . . Depending on your love partner for your feelings of self-worth is a major step in the wrong direction.

LoveNote. . . *It's okay to feel angry. It is not okay to be consumed with anger.* Anger is not something to be contained; it is something to be released. Express it with this caveat: consider the consequences of it power. Anger is something that can hurt if expressed with the intention to get even. Often we inflict our feelings of anger on the ones we love the most. Not a good idea. Everyone feels angry occasionally *and* everyone in the relationship feels its effect.

LoveNote. . . *Affirmation* ~ My love partner and I share a mutual commitment to hold aside no less than one evening each week; a purposely scheduled event, where we can be alone together. It is an evening that is sacred in that we allow nothing to disrupt our coming together as two best friends and lovers.

LoveNote. . . Being in the same room and talking; not running away. . . just talking about things that are important to the two of you, can be almost as much fun and as productive as foreplay.

LoveNote... What you take for granted disappears!

LoveNote. . . Maturity is the ability to live up to the responsibilities of a love relationship, and this means being dependable. It means keeping your word; it means living in your relationship as if your word really means something.

LoveNote. . . *For Men Only* ~ Never be someone your lover knows too well. In other words, let her know who you really are *and* always have there be more of you for her to discover. Never let it be predictable. Let it be spontaneous. Spontaneity demonstrates that you are paying attention to her and the relationship. This may help to keep her from feeling taken for granted. Be full of surprises; the kind of surprises you would want from your lover.

LoveNote. . . This is the solitary virtue of anger. *We become empowered by anger when we view it as something that brings to our awareness those parts of us that need healing.* There are other benefits worthy of discovery; only one virtue.

LoveNote... *Affirmation* ~ I have come to the realization that what is possible for me to become in my relationship only truly changes when I am willing to see what is impossible for me to continue being.

LoveNote... Commitment is a deep trust, a devotion discovered in the choice to be together. Commitment needs no agreements because it is based on desire, not obligation. A forever love relationship requires devotion, loyalty and a mature ability to commit.

LoveNote. . . *For Singles Only* ~ It could be said that one of the signs you may be ready for a committed relationship is when you reach a point where you've found someone you love and want to be with, yet you experience a feeling of hesitancy to relinquish the freedom you have also learned to love. It is the solitude of single life; a place where you learned to love who *you* are and be comfortable with that. It is proof that you know about discipline. To allow yourself a time of healing, a time to get to know *you*, is a wonderful gift; the same gift of love that now presents the challenge to step into the future, without holding on to the past. It is the first step you take while you are still afraid. It requires letting go of the need to be in a relationship and mastering the fear that keeps you from taking the first step to the next relationship; the singles' rite of passage. The reluctance to experience this ritual may come from a lack of conversations that construct the mutual commitment necessary to honor each other's right to be alone while you are together. A new freedom waits to be discovered; the freedom to be who you really are with the one you love.

LoveNote. . . A love relationship anchored in unconditional love can survive the roughest storm. Trust puts you in the same boat. . . side-by-side. . . working on learning to trust, and trusting. . . together! Trust has you both rowing in the same direction.

LoveNote. . . Oh, what fun to make great music together! However. . . no matter how carefully we work together to play the right lovenotes, our relationship sometimes plays sour notes; we strike a wrong chord. Love, commitment and loving conversation enables us to make music together in a way that helps us stay in tune with one another. Committed lovers listen for the music in words that come from the heart. The music of the heart is the nourishment of love. When two hearts make music together, it's as if the angels sing. Take care to always be singing the same song.

LoveNote. . . Our feelings help us to discover ourselves. Heed their call. They provide clues and insights into who we are and often become the catalyst for re-inventing ourselves. The energy for change is inspired by the emotional honesty we express through our feelings.

LoveNote. . . *Just because we know something doesn't mean anything.* Something can never really mean anything until we *do* something with it. We must do something - whatever it takes - to make our relationships the relationships we love being in. We must always carefully consider what action to take. Action without thought is only thoughtless action. That rarely works. Knowing this does not mean our relationships will always be great. We have choice. Every choice has a consequence. The dilemma is this: there are two people. That means we have two people making choices and there are a multitude of choices each of us could make. Each love partner is only and always responsible for their own choices. Relationships are individual projects first - the one with ourselves - and mutually beneficial projects second - the one with ourselves and our lover. Taking responsibility for our own stuff is a wonderful gift we give ourselves and our love partner. Relationships take our constant attention; every day and every minute. It is when we forget this that problems begin.

LoveNote... When in the heat of the battle, always remember: a warm hug cools a slow burn. It may be better to temporarily put aside feelings of anger during misunderstandings and express your love in a silent, close embrace. It is at times like these, when tempers are flaring, that words can not only fan the flames, they can be like a flash fire; once the fire rages through, there is not much of anything left. A hug at that moment, would be a shining example of unconditional love. Being angry doesn't mean you are no longer loved or lovable, or that you do not love your love partner. Love stands on its own. It only needs your constant attention if you want it to grow. While it may be difficult to express love in the middle of no agreement, it is possible. Imagine a relationship where love partners, in the midst of a disagreement, can agree to a truce long enough to again call attention to the single thing that keeps them together... love. Hold one another, if only for a moment. When things cool down, have a warm and loving conversation that again gives birth to the possibility of agreement. If you can imagine it, you can bring it to pass. What an exciting possibility! Love more quickly heals a slow burn.

LoveNote. . . Taking your forever lover for granted drives a wedge between the two of you. Then comes the drifting apart you once feared. You become lonely, anxious and withdrawn. What you take for granted, disappears! You and your lover may still be together physically, however, most likely neither one of you are really there for each other. To avoid the consequences of neglect, you will find that the only solution is the open talk you can allow yourself to have about it. Embrace your concerns. Sharing your true self with your love partner adds a new dimension to your relationship. Allowing your love partner to know your inner-world; to know how you really feel, is sharing at a higher level; perhaps even a spiritual level. You will discover a higher source of strength. Not being afraid of how your love partner will react is a true test of courage. Being willing to share yourself in this manner tells your lover the level of trust you are willing to express. When you lovingly communicate, the depth of connection that comes from this kind of intimate conversation, brings on a deeper experience of love, most desired yet difficult when you are inclined to withhold because of fear. You make the choice. Intimacy or separation. It is only and always in your hands. Talk or be silent and wait for the inevitable; the ultimate separation.

LoveNote. . . *Affirmation* ~ Forever is as far as we can go. The challenge is to both arrive there at the same time. . . together. Let's look upon our love relationship as a shared adventure; one that is a journey into the unknown. Let's imagine a journey on which we create our future, and our happiness together, in step. . . one loving step at a time.

Together. . . one of the keys to a successful and healthy love relationship. It is as simple as the concept of team. All the players on a team must learn to play together, in some sort of mutually acceptable and loving way.

Commitment is another important idea that is always certain to support the worthwhile notion of team. We can only and always be certain that those things we are committed to work on *together* will always have a stronger possibility of happening and a greater longevity when they happen.

We must be brave enough to pool our needs by sharing them with one another. We must then each let go of our expectations about how those needs get fulfilled. Love is as love does.

We must learn to honestly love the one we are with, with no expectations about how we feel the love need be returned. *Forever together* may be the reward.

With each love partner playing full-out, as a genuine member of the team, the trip becomes the romantic adventure we may have only dreamed about, yet never had the courage to take. It's two to the tenth power for starters. . . and it gets better. It takes two people who really love each other. . . *working together.*

We must avoid the temptation of side-trips; those times when we let our misguided thoughts get the best of us and we say something we wish we hadn't or any other side-trip that slows down progress. The temptation of side-trips is the plague along the journey. We do not have to participate.

The effect of team lends itself to letting go of which play each of us must make to win. Every play in the game is negotiated within the intention of the spirit of the team.

The game of love doesn't care *who* wins it. It knows that only committed team members *can* win it! It knows the thrill of victory and the agony of defeat. It knows that a victory shared is indeed the only victory.

If we want an extraordinary love relationship, we

must *be* someone who is extraordinary in the relationship. Extraordinary love partners give birth to extraordinary results.

With the maturity associated with the concept of team, comes the wisdom to understand that as long as both of us are playing on the same team. . . we may as well be on the *winning* team. That is the team that will take us to forever. *Imagine the possibilities!*

Special LoveNote for Singles Only!

LoveNote. . . *For Singles Only* ~ Trust your heart! It always tells the truth! When you have a concern that life is passing you by and you wonder why you haven't found your true love. . . that's your head speaking. It gets your attention by creating a worry about not finding anyone. Quit looking. That may be part of the problem. When your head talks it reflects what *you* think about the situation. Anxiety and fear feel right at home in the mind. They know they have no power other than what you give them. They know you sometimes aren't quite sure you know who does have the power. The heart knows the truth.

The beginning of the journey from the head to the heart is only *'a decision to begin it'* away. It begins when you become curious enough to self-inquire; to dig deep enough to discover what is in your heart; to discover what you didn't know you didn't know! Your heart will become open, active and brave.

Your head makes up things based upon what you already know. Often those are the things that haven't worked very well for you in the past. Often that's what keeps you stuck. It would have you think this journey is on a worrisome and fearful path.

The heart explores new ways of being. It helps you discover the possibility that love is. When love speaks from the heart, it gets your undivided attention with words of encouragement, understanding, courage, confidence and acceptance. You take notice.

Your head speaks out of both sides of its mouth. Commitment in a relationship demands dependability. Your head wobbles from one idea to another, with no particular focus. It can come up with more reasons 'not to' than it can good reasons to take the leap with faith and know you will be okay. It makes up fear so it doesn't have to risk taking the leap into the unknown. Part of the problem is it thinks it knows the unknown and it cannot know.

Words from the heart might sound like this:

> *"Remember to put me first! I am love. I will never let you down."*

> *"Listen to me! I will tell you when it's time to take the big step. I know you are still afraid. To step over into love, you must first walk through your fear. You can do it if you take my lead."*

"You are loving you more now. That's good. You are in process and being prepared to be somebody's 'favorite person to love.' Patience. This takes time. Soon you will be ready."

"You are beginning to discover genuine intimacy with yourself. Self-intimacy is good. Have patience. You're getting to know you better. Take it slow and steady. Easy now. You're doing very well."

"Remember, I am love. When you are ready to listen I will speak and you will know it's me speaking and you will know it's time."

How can you be sure you are really ready for a new relationship?

In your heart you will know it's time when you no longer feel the *need* to be in a relationship. . . *and* you are comfortable with that idea. That kind of love for yourself lights your heart-light. It makes you visible to others who have similar feelings. Your heart-light is loves' subtle, yet silent signal. It lights the path to love. Proudly and fearlessly let it shine.

The next seemingly logical dilemma is: Where do I look? That's your head talking again.

Do life! Live fully! *Be* wherever you show up! Really *be* who you are wherever you go. Make certain your 'best foot forward' is really who you are and not someone you think someone else thinks you *should* be. "Where do I look?" comes from fear. It makes you think that you need to be looking.

It is not necessary to look. Only pay attention. Put yourself in loves' way. Be active where other people are. Remember: Like attracts like! Let your heart-light shine.

You won't find him or her. . . you will find each other. When need disappears, choice shows up! Not needing to be in a relationship with someone creates the freedom to choose to be in a relationship with someone. In your heart you will know. . . it's time.

When you learn to really love yourself, your energy is focused on love not fear, which often appears as desperation. Redirect your energy to listen to the healthy and truthful messages of the heart. Thus begins the journey from the head to the heart.

Only trust your heart! It only and always tells the truth!

LoveNote From the Author's Heart. . . We get pretty much what we expect to get in our relationship. What we expect to get is what we focus on. If it turns out good, we should not be disappointed. If it turns out bad, we should not be disappointed. We got what we expected. What else did we expect to get? Perhaps we should learn to be in a relationship with no expectations. In a spirit of unity, only and always work together, all the time, to create the best relationship we can. All the time. With intention. In a spirit of unity. *All the time.* If we could do that, maybe we wouldn't have to be concerned about expectations when they surface; we would know things were always going to be as good as the people working on them. Perhaps that is why it is important to have a great relationship with ourselves. When we can do a great relationship with ourselves, we can do a great relationship with two people. When we reach that place, we can have a great relationship with someone else because we already know how to *be* in a great relationship. . . with ourselves!

LoveNote. . . The miracle of unconditional love is nurtured by the power of the Divine and our own imagination. *Imagine the possibilities!*

"Burst of truth, flashes of insight and words of wisdom for those on the path to wholesome and healthy love relationships. A thought-provoking, refreshing adventure in love and self-discovery. A must-read book for all!"

John Gray, Ph.D., Author
Men Are From Mars, Women Are From Venus &
What Your Mother Couldn't Tell You and Your Father Didn't Know

"How to Really Love the One You're With" is a revealing and personally empowering look at self-liberating insights that will assist you in achieving a healthy love relationship anchored in unconditional love. Its' wisdom will inspire you to deeper levels of self-acceptance and understanding. These words of love will benefit anyone; married or single; whether couples already in a committed relationship or singles who may be in search of a healthy love relationship.

Larry James has transformed words of love into a message of hope that offers encouragement, inspiration and the opportunity for enlightenment in relationships. He presents a priceless treasury of inspiring and insightful thoughts, ideas, indispensable guidelines and reflections on how to really love the one you're with.

"How to Really Love You're With" is available at bookstores or for a personally autographed copy call 800 725-9223. Visa or MasterCard accepted.

How to *Really* Love the One You're With
(Paperback).......................**$14.95**
ISBN 1-881558-02-9
Price does not include shipping and handling.

Coming Soon. . .

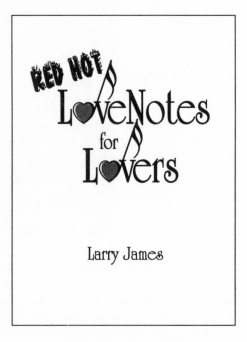

More **LoveNotes** that take a candid peek at two
hearts dancing together in the bedroom; a look at
the sexual side of healthly love relationships! Look
for it at your favorite book store!

About
Larry James. . .

Larry James is founder and President of the Career Assurance Network. At age 10 he made his first sales call. He's been networking, both personally and professionally, and sharing his experience with others ever since. He was in broadcasting for twelve years and was a popular radio personality in the 1960's and early 1970's.

His purpose is: *"Helping others help themselves."* He is committed to sharing ideas and information that will assist anyone interested in improving the quality of their life. He has authored several books and audio cassette programs to assist in that process.

He is a professional speaker and author. He has earned his reputation as a speaker and workshop leader by teaching success principles and techniques he has learned and developed from his experiences in the field of broadcasting, selling and from his seminars and workshops. He fully acknowledges his responsibility to practice what he teaches; inspiring others by example.

He is a student of Truth and consistently studies and shares success strategies about personal and business relationships. He champions the value of personal and business networking and has been called the "Guru of Networking." He travels nationally leading seminars, workshops and presenting keynotes of inspiration that focus on personal and professional relationship development.

Puzzled. . . about relationships??

Sometimes the pieces don't fit together so well. . .

sometimes they do!

Now Available In Your Area!

A workshop designed to help you fit the pieces of the relationship puzzle together in a healthy way.

How to *Really* Love the One You're With!

A Relationship Enrichment LoveShop™
Featuring
Larry James, Professional Speaker/Author

"How to *Really* Love the One You're With" is an interactive workshop experience from the LoveShop Series™. Each LoveShop is a place where people who are committed to having excellence in their relationships can freely and openly discuss the various pieces of the relationship puzzle. It will assist you in learning more of how to really *love* the one you're with and really *live* with the one you love!

Topics open for discussion. . .

Unconditional Love • Self-Love • Trust • Acceptance • Choice • Interpretation • Commitment • Fun & Frolic • Making Love • Forgiveness • Communications •

Understanding • Misunderstandings • Romantic Myths • Creating Space • Mutual Support • Thoughtfulness • Letting Go • Spirituality... *and anything else that comes up!*

About your LoveShop leader...

Larry James, Professional Speaker and Author. Larry leads personal and professional relationship development seminars and workshops nationally. The LoveShop is based upon his best selling book, **"How to *Really* Love the One You're With!"** Larry will share his personal experience that led to the writing of his book. He will lead a lively discussion with the audience that reflects healthy attitudes about love relationships. Dr. Larry Losoncy, Ph.D., Marriage and Family Therapist, occasionally joins Larry James as co-leader at the LoveShops.

About the book that inspired the LoveShop...

"Bursts of truth, flashes of insight and words of wisdom for those on the path to wholesome and healthy love relationships. A thought-provoking, refreshing adventure in love and self-discovery. A must-read book for all!"

Dr. John Gray, Ph.D., Author
Men Are From Mars, Women Are From Venus &
What Your Mother Couldn't Tell You &
Your Father Didn't Know

The Possibilities of the LoveShop for you and your friends...

The LoveShop presents guidelines for healthy love relationships. It's for *together lovers... husbands, wives and committed lovers;* those who have found their true love. It's for *love partners whose love has grown cold;* those who would like to recapture the excitement that brought them together in the beginning. It's for *lovers in waiting;* those who are alone, no longer lonely and ready for a committed relationship or at least interested in one. It also works well for people who have experienced the pain of a relationship that didn't work and who desire to experience the healing that comes from the intention to recovery fully.

The Relationship Enrichment LoveShop is presented nationally and is available in your area. If your organization, church, married or singles group would like to be a part of this "tell-it-like-it-is" LoveShop in your own hometown, call toll-free 800 725-9223 for complete details.

About Career Assurance Network. . .

Career Assurance Network is a company specializing in personal and professional relationship development seminars, workshops and keynote addresses.

Career Assurance Network, whose acronym is CAN, is committed to providing services and products that will assist you in being the best you CAN be! Larry's books and audio learning systems are available from the publishing arm of our network, Career Assurance Press.

About Life$kills Learning Systems. . .

A complete list of Larry's audio learning systems, books and other products is available upon request.

If you are interested in a list of available seminar or keynote topics or in contacting Larry to arrange a personal appearance, please write to the address below or call our toll-free number.

Larry James would love to hear from you!

If this book, or any other works of the author have made a difference in your life or if you have ideas you would like to contribute, please take a moment and let him know. Send all correspondence to the address below.

Larry James
Career Assurance Network
P.O. Box 12695
Scottsdale, Arizona 85267-2695

602 998-9411 ~ 602 998-2173 Fax ~ 800 725-9223
Online: CANetwork1@aol.com